musicroom® PRESENTS

HITS OF THE YEAR

Wise Publications
part of The Music Sales Group
London / New York / Paris / Sydney / Copenhagen / Berlin / Madrid / Hong Kong / Tokyo

Published by
Musicroom
14-15 Berners Street, London W1T 3LJ, UK.

Exclusive Distributors:
Music Sales Limited
Distribution Centre, Newmarket Road,
Bury St Edmunds, Suffolk IP33 3YB, UK.

Music Sales Pty Limited
Units 3-4, 17 Willfox Street, Condell Park, NSW 2200, Australia.

Order No. MRM017
ISBN: 978-1-78038-897-7

Edited by Jenni Norey.
Cover photos by 2012 Dave M. Benett/Getty Images, Jon Furniss/Wire Image,
PA Wire/Press Association Images, Startraks Photo/Rex Features.

Printed in the EU.

ALONE AGAIN ALYSSA REID 5

BORN TO DIE LANA DEL REY 10

BRIGHT LIGHTS TINCHY STRYDER FEAT. PIXIE LOTT 17

CALL MY NAME CHERYL 24

DOMINO JESSIE J 32

DRUNK ED SHEERAN 38

MAMA DO THE HUMP RIZZLE KICKS 44

ONE THING ONE DIRECTION 52

PAYPHONE MAROON 5 FEAT. WIZ KHALIFA 62

PICKING UP THE PIECES PALOMA FAITH 68

SIMPLY AMAZING TREY SONGZ 57

WE ARE YOUNG FUN 72

WIDE AWAKE KATY PERRY 78

WINGS LITTLE MIX 84

Alone Again

Words & Music by Tom Kelly, Billy Steinberg,
Raynford Humphreys, Alyssa Reid & Jamie Appleby

B♭m G♭ D♭ A♭
1. Yeah, I think a-bout you all the time. Tell my friends that I'll be fine, but they know that I'd be ly-in'. Do my
(2.) out with oth-er girls and no, it ain't the same. And I still turn my head ev-'ry time I hear your name.
B♭m G♭ D♭ A♭
best to get you out of my head. And I'll be try'n' to fake a smile through my days, though in-side I'm stead-y dy-ing. Uh.
Star-ing at the phone can make some-bod-y go in-sane. So I'm hang-ing at the club try'n-a drink a-way the pain. Uh.
B♭m G♭ D♭ A♭
Back in Shot town ev-'ry-thing re-mind-ed me. I turn on the ra-di-o and e-ven mu-sic haunts me.
This a night-mare, tell me when I'm wak-ing up. I re-gret the day that I de-cid-ed we were break-ing up.
B♭m G♭ A♭sus4 A♭
I know I told you this and I told you that but the bot-tom line is, ba-by girl I want you back.
With-out mak-ing up e-ven though the minds are stacked, bot-tom line is, ba-by girl I need you back.

B♭m G♭ D♭ A♭
When you said I could move on and go, you said I'm weak and it shows; I could-n't go on with-out you.
B♭m G♭ D♭
N.C.
Now I'm sit-ting in this house a-lone won-d'rin' why I left home and I'm hop-ing that you know that:
B♭m G♭ D♭ A♭ B♭m G♭
Till now I al-ways got by on my own. I nev-er real-ly
D♭ A♭ B♭m G♭ D♭ A♭
cared un-til I met you. And now it chills me to the bone.

1.
2.
D♭/F G♭ A♭sus4 A♭ A♭sus4 A♭
How do I get you a - lone?
2. I've been
B♭m G♭ A♭ B♭m G♭
8vb till *
I won-der where you are to-night. No an-swer on the tel-e-phone.
A♭ G♭ D♭/F E♭m7
And the night goes by so ver-y slow. Oh I
8vb
G♭ D♭/F E♭m7 A♭sus4 A♭ D♭
hope that it won't end though, a - lone.
8vb

N.C.
B♭m G♭
*
And I'm hop - ing that you know that: Till now I
D♭ A♭ B♭m G♭ D♭ A♭
al - ways got by on my own. I nev - er real - ly cared un - til I met you.
B♭m G♭ D♭ A♭ D♭/F G♭
And now it chills me to the bone. How do I get you a - lone?
A♭sus4 A♭ D♭/F G♭ A♭
How do I get you a - lone?

Born To Die

Words & Music by Elizabeth Grant & Justin Parker

C
Em
D
breaks ev-'ry step that I take,
but I'm hop-ing at the gates, they'll tell me that you're mine.
G
D
G
2. Walk-ing through the cit - y streets,
is it by mis-take or de - sign?
3. Lost but now I am found.
I can see but once I was blind.
D
C
Em
I feel so a - lone on a Fri - day night.
Can you make it feel like
I was so con - fused as a lit - tle child.
Tried to take what I could

D
home, if I tell you you're mine? It's like I told you hon - ey:
get. Scared that I could - n't find all the ans - wers, hon - ey
C
Em
D
Don't make me sad, don't make me cry. Some-times love is not e -
C
Em
-nough and the road gets tough, I don't know why. Keep mak-ing me laugh. Let's go get high.

D
C
The road is long, we car - ry on. Try to have fun in the mean - time. Come and take a walk on the wild side.
Em
D
C
Let me kiss you hard in the pour-ing rain. You like your girls in - sane.
Em
D
Choose your last words. This is the last time, 'cause you and

1.
2.
C
N.C.
I, we were born to die.
Em
D
C
We were born to die.
We were born to die.
Em
Am
Em
Come and take a walk on the wild side.
Let me kiss you hard in the pour-ing
D
C
Em
rain. You like your girls in - sane.
Don't make me sad, don't make me cry.

D
C
Some-times love is not e - nough and the road gets tough, I don't know why. Keep mak-ing me laugh.
Em
D
C
Let's go get high. The road is long, we car - ry on. Try to have fun in the mean-
Em
- time. Come and take a walk on the wild side. Let me kiss you hard in the pour - ing
D
C
rain. You like your girls in - sane. Choose your last words.

Em
D
C
N.C.
This is the last time, 'cause you and I, we were born to die.
C
Em
G
C
Em
G
C
Em
D

Bright Lights

Words & Music by Jarrad Rogers,
Kwasi Danquah & Pixie Lott

F♯ C♯ G♯m D♯m F♯ B
Uh, uh! From the
G♯m D♯m F♯ C♯
ground to the sky, and it was-n't o - ver - night. Strydes.
B C♯ D♯m
1. Last time run-ning nev - er went too well. Heart say - ing car-ry on, head's tell - ing me for - feit.
(2.) love me or hate me? There's no pleas-ing ev-'ry-bod-y. Need to fo-cus then he lost track, I'm real-ly sor-ry.

F♯
C♯
4fr
Glimpse of the high life, I wish I nev-er saw this. Now I want it all... I'm self - ish.
Left the black clouds, bright lights got me feel-ing jol - ly. Nev-er let you down, that's my word you ain't got-ta wor-ry.
B
C♯
D♯m
6fr
Felt locked down like I caught a death sen-tence, like A-lan Su-gar fi-red me from The Ap-pren-tice.
Work for this, don't know a-bout you but I work for this. Cou-ple la-bels said I was-n't
See my lit-tle weight, I must-'ve lost half. E-ven Nan-do's won't send me a new black card.
worth the risk. Just an-oth-er hood-rat hood-ie with a black hat. He's just one of them look-ing for a
And there's all o-pin-ions and as-sump-tions. Back to the grind and there's more where it comes from.
purse to nick. Nev-er real-ly had a plan B. Stayed on point, I am sharper than a Stan-ley.

F♯
C♯
4fr
I love the life 'cause my life flash col-ours on. Tell Cher-yl Cole and Ri-han-na that I love them.
Big__ star, flash car, look-ing trend-y. Mi-nogue on my list I ain't talk-ing 'bout Ky - lie.
B
C♯
4fr
D♯m
6fr
From young I've been ob-sessed with the fame. Know you're in lane 'cause your dreams were the same.
F♯
C♯
4fr
Ev-'ry day I prayed, real-ly wish-ing for a change. Dreams to re-al-i-ty and now I'm in the game.__
G♯m
4fr
D♯m
6fr
F♯
B
Flash lights__ and the good life,__ keep call-ing out__ my name, and I

G♯m D♯m F♯ C♯ G♯m D♯m
4fr 6fr 4fr 4fr 6fr
pray some - how some-thing's gon-na change.
Bright lights in the sky - line won't
F♯ B G♯m D♯m
4fr 6fr
let me lose my way, 'cause I know some - how some-thing's gon - na change.
1. 2.
F♯ C♯ F♯ C♯
4fr 4fr
2. Show me how you feel. Do you
Yeah.
Let me tell you when to

B F♯ B
take it down. This is the part where the song breaks down. Stay look-ing up, nev-er
(Backing vocal ad lib.)
F♯ C♯
fac-ing down. Long as the bright lights are blaz-ing down. Oh,
G♯m D♯m F♯ B G♯m D♯m F♯ C♯
ah… Oh, ooh. Ah!
G♯m D♯m F♯ B
Flash lights and the good life, keep call-ing out my name, and I
(Vocal ad lib.)

G♯m D♯m F♯ C♯
4fr 6fr 4fr
pray some - how some-thing's gon - na change.
G♯m D♯m F♯ B
4fr 6fr
Bright lights in the sky - line, let me lose my way, 'cause I
G♯m D♯m F♯ C♯
4fr 6fr 4fr
know some - how some-thing's gon - na change.
B C♯ D♯m F♯ C♯
4fr 6fr 4fr
Ey, ooh...

Call My Name

Words & Music by Adam Wiles

Cm7
Bbadd4/Eb
Ab
Cm7
Bbadd4/Eb
-fused_ by the way I change. How d'you think I feel when you call my__
Ab
Cm7
Bbadd4/Eb
name,__ my name? Say my name ba - by.
C5
1.
Ab5
2.
Ab5
1. Yes, I

C5
3fr
A♭5
4fr
love you say for the way I know we've been a - part. (...part, part, part...) It's an
end - less cir - cle, a poi - son ar - row to my heart. (...heart, heart, heart...) Say - in'
I, I love what you do to me, need you to stay with me.
A♭
I, I love you too much to let go.

A♭
Cm7
B♭add4/E♭
How d'you think I feel when you call my
A♭
Cm7
B♭add4/E♭
A♭
name? You got me con - fused by the way I change. How d'you think I
Cm7
B♭add4/E♭
A♭
Cm7
B♭add4/E♭
feel when you call my name, my name? Say my name ba - by.

N.C.
C5
3fr
2. It's the con - stant thought of my ba - by tak - ing up my
A♭5
4fr
C5
3fr
time.__ (...time,__ time,__ time...)__ It's a non - stop vi - sion of
you that's play - ing on my mind.__ (...mind,__

A♭5
C5
mind, mind...) Say - in' I, I
love what you do to me, need you to stay with me. I,
A♭5
C5
I love you too much to let go.
A♭

A♭
Cm7
B♭add4/E♭
A♭
How d'you think I feel when you call my name? You got me con-
Cm7
B♭add4/E♭
A♭
-fused by the way I change. How d'you think I
Cm7
B♭add4/E♭
A♭
Cm7
B♭add4/E♭
feel when you call my name, my name? Say my name ba-by.

A♭
Cm7
B♭add4/E♭
(Oh, oh, oh...) When you call my
name.
(Oh, oh, oh, oh, oh, oh, oh...)
(Oh,
oh, oh...) When you call my name.
(Oh, oh, oh, oh, oh, oh, oh...)
Say my name, ba - by!

Domino

Words & Music by Max Martin, Lukasz Gottwald,
Claude Kelly, Jessica Cornish & Henry Russell Walter

G
Gsus4
G
Gsus4
-plode.
-tar.
I can taste the ten-sion like a cloud of
G
Gsus4
smoke in the air. Now I'm breath-ing like I'm run-ning 'cause you're tak-ing me there. Don't you know:
G
Gsus4
G
Gsus4
you spin me out of con-trol. Ooh, ooh, ooh, ooh.
C
Am
Em
D7
We can do this all night. Turn this club, skin tight. Ba-by, come on.

C
Am
Ooh, ooh, ooh, ooh. Boom-ing like a bass drum. Spark-in' up a
Em
D7
C
Am
rhy - thm. Ba - by, come on! Ooh, ooh, ooh, ooh. Rock my world
Em
D7
in - to the sun - light. Make this dream the best I've ev - er known.
C
Am
Em
D7
Dirt - y danc - ing in the moon - light. Take me down

C
Am
like I'm a do-mi-no. Ev-'ry se-cond is a high-light.
Em
D7
C
Am
When we touch don't ev-er let me go. Dirt-y danc-
Em
D7
-ing in the moon-light. Take me down like I'm a do-mi-no.
1.
G
Gsus4
G
Gsus4
2. You got me los-ing my

2.
C
Am
Em
D7
Ooh, ba - by, ba - by, got me feel - ing so right. Ooh, ba - by, ba - by, danc -
C
Am
- ing in the moon - light. Ooh, ba - by, ba - by, got me feel - ing so right.
1.
Em
D7
2.
Em
D7
N.C.
Ooh, ba - by, ba - by, danc - ing in the moon - light. Ooh, ba - by, ba - by... Ooh, ooh, ooh, ooh.
C
Am
Em
D7
Rock my world in - to the sun - light. Make this dream

C
Am
the best I've ev - er known. Dirt - y dancing in the moon - light.
Em
D7
C
Am
Take me down like I'm a do mi- no. Ev - 'ry se - condis a high - light.
Em
D7
C
Am
When we touch don't ev - er let me go. Dirt - y danc-
Em
D7
- ing in the moon - light. Take me down like I'm a do - mi - no.

Drunk

Words & Music by Ed Sheeran & Jake Gosling

C
did - n't kill me, it nev - er made me strong - er at all.
though I know you'll nev - er love me like you used to.
G
Love will scar your make up. Lips sticks to me, so now I may - be lean
There may be oth - er peo - ple like us who see the flick - er of a clip - per when they light up.
Em
back there. I'm sat here wish - ing I was so - ber.
Flames just cre - ate us but burns don't heal like be - fore.

C
I know I'll nev - er hold you like I used to.
And you don't hold me an - y - more.
G
But a
On
Em
G
house gets cold when you cut the heat - ing. With-out you to hold I'll be freez - ing.
cold days cold plays out like the band's name. I know I can't heal things with a hand - shake.
Em
G
Can't re - ly on my heart to beat in 'cause you take parts of it ev - 'ry eve - ning.
You know I can change, as I be - gan say-ing. You cut me wide o - pen like land - scape.

Em
G
Take words out of my mouth just from breath - ing. Re - place with phra - ses like "When you leav - ing
O - pen bot-tles of beer, but nev - er cham - pagne, to ap-plaud you with the sound that my hands make.
C
me?" Should I? Should I? May - be I'll get
Em
G
Em
drunk a - gain. I'll be drunk a -
G
Em
G
- gain, I'll be drunk a - gain to feel a lit - tle

C
D
love.
Em
G
All by my - self,
I'm here a - gain.
Em
G
All by my - self,
you know I'll nev - er change.
Em
G
All by my - self,

C
Em
all by my - self. I'm just
Em
G
Em
drunk a - gain. I'll be drunk a -
G
Em
G
- gain, I'll be drunk a - gain to feel a lit - tle
C
D
love.

Mama Do The Hump

Words & Music by Norman Cook, Harley Alexander-Sule
& Jordan Stephens

3
(Rush past.) Like you've for-got-ten your mind or the driv-ers all up in your face, like "Can I see your buss pass?"
(Huh, na.) We just wan-na lick-le rhyme bruv, call me what you want but you should not call it a night, love.
And I might just join the mi-le high club, on-ly prob-lem be-ing that I could-n't give a fly-ing f**k!
Yeah, lem-me touch back down slap her on the bum un-til it comes back 'round.

Half the room's like "Oi, what's this all a-bout?" with the oth-er half jiv-ing, I love that sound.
G
Ah-yeah, yeah I love that sound a yeah yeah I love that sound
So flick your fag butts at once on a mad one, like yeah, your ma-ma can hump.
G
Ma-ma do the hump, ma-ma do the hump, hump. Ma-ma won't you please let me do the hump, hump.

To Coda
Ma-ma do the hump, ma-ma do the hump, hump.
Ma-ma won't you please let me do the hump, hump.
Yo, it's been a long week, how I've got this much en - er - gy is be-yond me.
I just want all of these girls to be on me and may-be e - ven one of them could be Be-yon - cé.
We ain't gon - na pack that rap noise in all of that chee - sy stuff; clap, clap, sing.

And we're gon - na burn some ca - lo - ries right here, right now. Ain't o - ver till a fat boy slims, ma - ma...
Ma - ma do the hump, ma - ma do the hump, hump. Ma - ma won't you please let me do the hump, hump.
Ma - ma do the hump, ma - ma do the hump, hump. Ma - ma won't you please let me do the hump, hump.
Yeah, knock a rum back down, bust a lit - tle jig - gy as the drum track pounds.

D.S. al Coda
Half the room_ are just mak-ing their own crowd with the oth-er half jiv-ing, I love that sound.
Coda
G
Ma-ma won't you please let me do the hump, hump. When we step in-to a room ev-'ry-bod-y makes a path-way,
'cause you know R K make the dance change. And we rule that crowd
and we don't change pace at the half way. We, we keep it mov-ing, we, we hold it down.

Can't stop, break sweat, no los - ing. Yes, no - bod - y gon - na take my crown. Hold
back. Na na, na na, nev - er gon - na hap - pen. (Go back.) Na na, na na, nev - er gon - na hap - pen.
Es - pec - ial - ly when it's all packed out, crowd shout - ing out yeah, I love that sound.
Ah - yeah, yeah I love that sound. Ah - yeah, yeah I love that sound.

So flick_ your fag butts at once on a mad one, like yeah,_ your ma-ma can hump.
G
Ma-ma do the hump, ma-ma do the hump, hump.
Ma-ma won't you please let me do the hump, hump.
Ma-ma do the hump, ma-ma do the hump, hump.
Ma-ma won't you please let me do the hump, hump.
G

One Thing

Words & Music by Carl Falk, Yami Racoub
& Savan Cotecha

D A D D A G
2. Shot me out of the sky. You're my kryp - to - nite.
3. Now I'm climb-ing the walls, but you don't notice at all, That
G A Bm G A D
You keep mak-ing me weak. Yeah, fro - zen and can't breathe. Some -
I'm go-ing out of my mind all day and all night. Some -
G D Bm A
- thing's got-ta give now, 'cause I'm dy - ing just to make you see. That I need
- thing's got-ta give now. 'cause I'm dy - ing just to know your name. And I need
G D G N.C.
you here with me now. 'Cause you've got that one thing.
you here with me now. 'Cause you've got that one thing.
So

D G A D Bm G A D
get out, get out, get out of my head and fall in - to my arms in - stead.
G A Bm G
1.
A D
I don't, I don't, don't know what it is, but I need that one thing. And
Bm A D D A D
you've got that one thing.
2.
A D D G A D Bm G
one thing. So get out, get out, get out of my mind and come on, come in - to

A D G A Bm
my life.__ I don't, I don't, don't know what it is,__ but
G A D Bm A D
I need__ that one thing._ And you've got__ that one__ thing. Oh,__
G Bm D A
oh,__ oh…
G Bm D A
You've got__ that one thing._

D G A D Bm G A D
Get out, get out, get out of my head and fall in - to my arms in - stead. So
D G A D Bm G A D
get out, get out, get out of my head and fall in - to my arms in - stead.
get out, get out, get out of my mind and come on, come in - to my life.
G A Bm G
I don't, I don't, don't know what it is, but I need that one
1.
A D
thing. So
2.
A D Bm A D
one thing. And you've got that one thing.

Simply Amazing

Words & Music by Tremaine Neverson, Christopher Umana
& Najja McDowell

F
Am7
-ers and all I feel is skin. I slow-ly kiss your face.
-set and the o-cean is her hair. What she do ain't fair.
C
F
Beau-ti-ful in ev-'ry way. You are.
But she knows me bet-ter than I know my-self.
See, I'm a
C
man that don't be-lieve in much. But I'll be damned
F
if I don't be-lieve in us.
Like how we play a
Like when I said I

Am7
fight up in the bath-room. Next thing you know I'm mak-ing love to you, girl.
love you for the first time. And the tears dropped from your eyes, girl.
C/E
Bb
Prom-ise me you'll nev - er change.
Don't you ev - er change.
She ain't per -
C
F
- fect but she's worth it. Ev-'ry breath I breathe for the life
Am7
of me. And I know I might not de-serve it but she

F
C
loves me. And it's sim-ply a-maz-ing. (You
F
are.) Sim-ply a-maz-ing. (You are.) Sim-ply a-maz-
Am7
1.
To Coda
F
-ing. And she loves me.
C5
3fr
And it's sim-ply a-maz-ing. A-maz-in', 'maz-ing.

2.
B♭
C
loves me. There is noth - ing in this world that can keep
F
G
Am7
me a - way from you. And there's no - bod - y
F
G
D.S. al Coda
who could ev - er com - pare to you. She ain't per -
Coda
B♭
N.C.
loves me. And it's sim-ply a - maz - ing.

Payphone

Words & Music by Adam Levine, Johan Schuster, Benjamin Levin,
Ammar Malik, Daniel Omelio & Cameron Thomaz

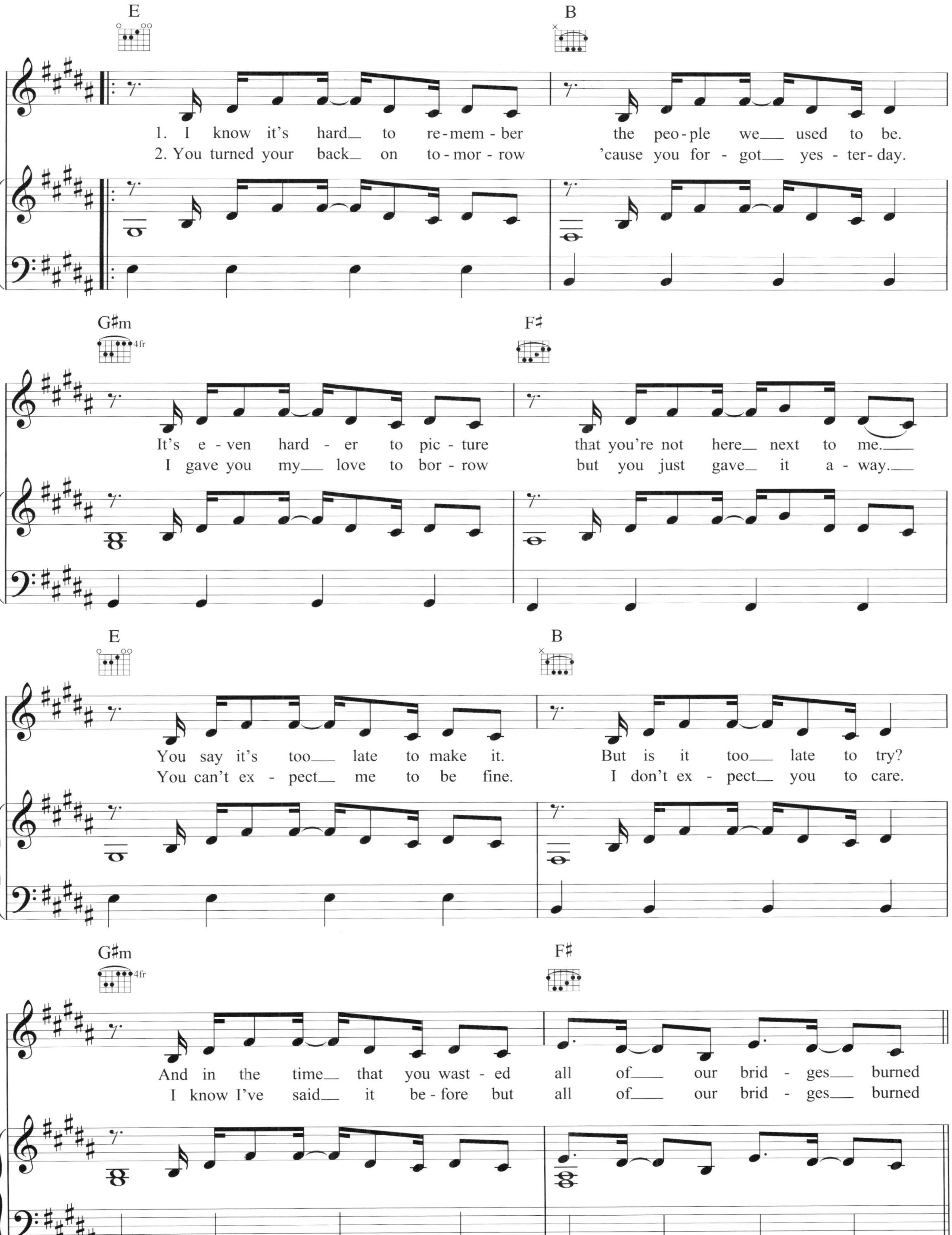
E
B
1. I know it's hard to re-mem-ber the peo-ple we used to be.
2. You turned your back on to-mor-row 'cause you for-got yes-ter-day.
G♯m
F♯
It's e-ven hard-er to pic-ture that you're not here next to me.
I gave you my love to bor-row but you just gave it a-way.
E
B
You say it's too late to make it. But is it too late to try?
You can't ex-pect me to be fine. I don't ex-pect you to care.
G♯m
F♯
And in the time that you wast-ed all of our brid-ges burned
I know I've said it be-fore but all of our brid-ges burned

E B G♯m
down. down. I've wast - ed my nights. You turned out the lights. Now I'm pa - ra -
F♯ E B G♯m
-lysed. Still stuck in that time when we called it love. But e - ven the sun sets in pa - ra -
F♯ E B
- dise. I'm at a pay - phone try - in' to call home. All of my change
G♯m F♯ E
I spent on you. Where have the times gone? Ba - by, it's all
4fr

B
G♯m
F♯
— wrong. Where are the plans — we made — for two? — If hap-py ev-er
E
B
G♯m
af-ter — did — ex-ist — I would still be hold-ing — you — like this. —
F♯
E
B
— All those fai-ry-tales are — full — of sh... — One more f**k-in'
G♯m
To Coda
1.
2.
F♯
love-song, — I'll — be sick. — — Now I'm at a pay-

N.C.
Man, f**k that...
phone.
I'll be out spend-ing all this mon-ey while you're sit-tin' 'round
won-der- in' why it was-n't you who came up from noth- in'. Made it from the bot-tom now when you see me I'm stunt-in'.
And all of my cars come with the push of a but- ton. Tell- in' me the chanc-es I blew up or what-ev-er you call it.
Switched my num-ber to my phone so you could nev-er call it. Don't need my name on my shirt, you can tell I'm ball- in'.

E
B
Swish, what a shame, could-'ve got picked. Had a real-ly good game but you missed your last
Phan-tom pull up, va-let o-pen doors. Wish you'd go a-way, got what you was look-in' for.
G♯m
shot. When you talk a-bout who you see at the top or
Now it's me who they want so you can take that
1.
F♯
what you could-'ve saw but sad to say it's o-ver for.
2.
F♯
D.S. al Coda
lit-tle piece of sh...with you. I'm at a pay-
Coda
F♯
N.C.
Now I'm at a pay-phone.

Picking Up The Pieces

Words & Music by Wayne Hector, Timothy Powell
& Paloma Faith

C
G
face do you see? Do you wish I was a bit more like
it used to be? And I have changed this room a-round more of - ten late-
D/F♯
Em
her? Am I too loud? I play the clown to cov - er up
- ly. It's clear that me and these four walls still know it's hers
C
Cm
C
Em
all these doubts.
and yours.
Per - fect heart. She's flaw - less.
D
G/D
C
Em
She's the oth - er wom - an shin - ing in her splen - dour.

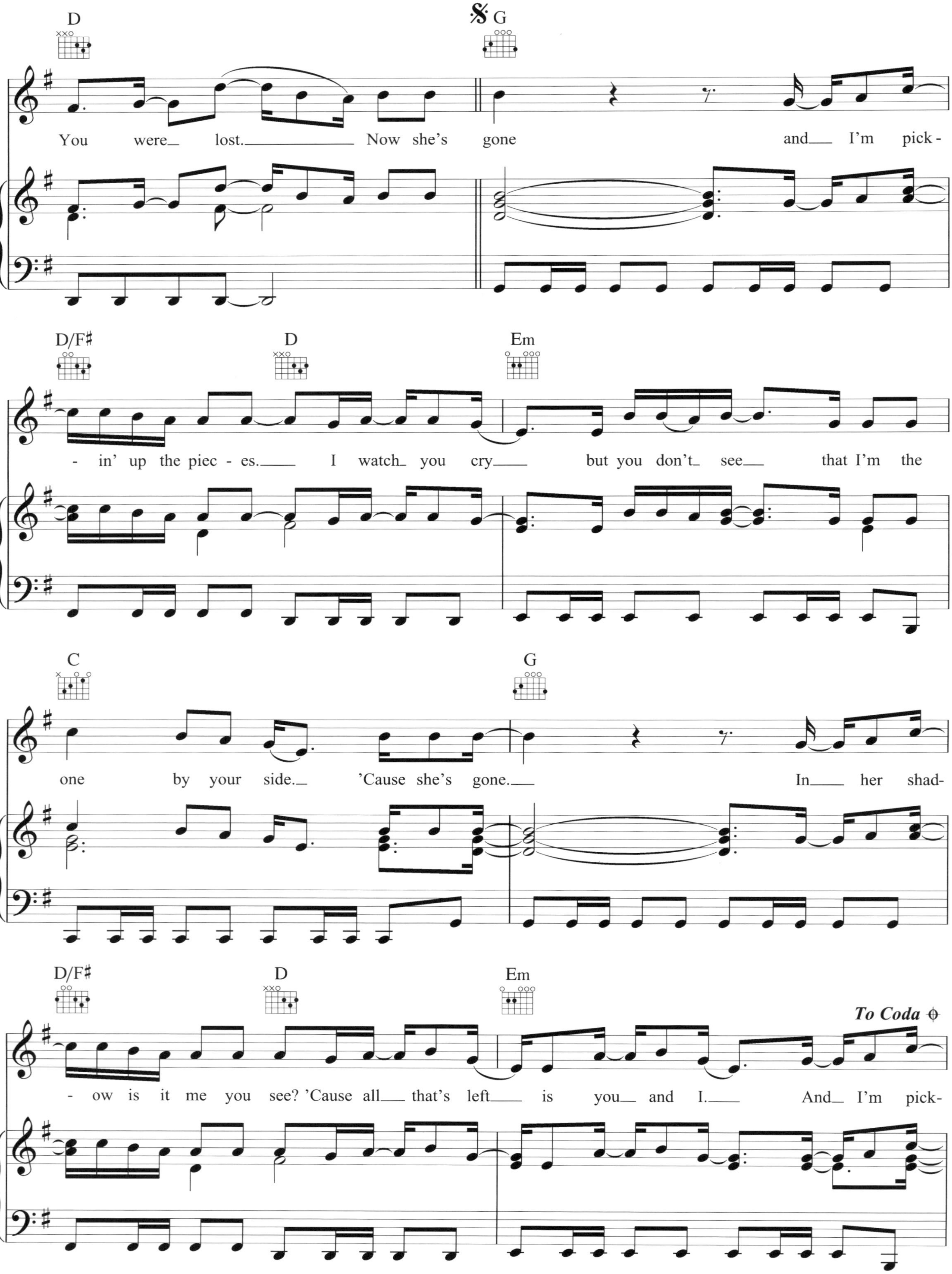
D
G
You were lost. Now she's gone and I'm pick-
D/F♯
D
Em
-in' up the piec-es. I watch you cry but you don't see that I'm the
C
G
one by your side. 'Cause she's gone. In her shad-
D/F♯
D
Em
To Coda
-ow is it me you see? 'Cause all that's left is you and I. And I'm pick-

C
1.
C5
3fr
-in' up the piec-es she left be-hind. 2. I found a pho-
2.
D/F♯
G
C(sus2)
Are we li-ars in de-ni-al? Are we smoke with-out the fire?
Em
D/F♯
G
D(sus4)
D.S. al Coda
Tell me please, is this worth it? I de-seve it. 'Cause she's
Coda
C
Em7
C(sus2)
Cm
3fr
G
-in' up the piec-es she left be-hind.

We Are Young

Words & Music by Jeff Bhasker, Nate Ruess,
Andrew Dost & Jack Antonoff

B♭
C7
F
ta - ken by some sun - glass - es ask - ing 'bout a scar. And I know I gave it to you months a - go.
Dm7
Gm
I know you're try - ing to for - get. But be - tween the drinks and sub - tle things the
B♭
C7
holes in my a - po - lo - gies, you know, I'm try - ing hard to take it back. So if by the
Much slower ♩ = 90
Gm
Am
Dm
C
B♭
C
time the bar clo - ses and you feel like fall - ing down I'll car - ry you home. To -

F
F/E
Dm7
- night
we are young.
C/E F B♭
B♭/D
B♭
So let's set the world on fi - re.
We can burn bright - er than the sun.
1.
2.
F/C
C
F/C
C
To Coda
(1º only)
To -
2. Now I

F
F/E
Dm7
know that I'm not all that you got. I guess that I, I just thought
C/E
F
Gm
3fr
may-be we could find new ways to fall a-part. But our friends are back,
B♭9
B♭
rit.
C
D.S. al Coda
(with repeat)
so let's raise a toast. 'Cause I found some-one to car-ry me home. To-
Coda
F
B♭
F/A
C/E
Car-ry me home to-night. Just car-ry me home to-night.
(Na na, na na na na, na na, na na na na, na na, na na na na, na na, na na na na.)

F
B♭
F/A
The world is on my side, I have no rea-son to run. So will some-one come and
C/E
F
B♭
car-ry me home to-night. The an-gels nev-er ar-rived but I can hear the choir.
F/A
C/E
F
so will some-one come and car-ry me home. To-night
F/E
Dm7
C/E
F
we are young. So let's set the world on

B♭ B♭/D B♭ F/C C
fi - re. We can burn brigh - ter than the sun. To-
F F/E Dm7 C/E F
-night we are young. So let's set the world on
B♭ B♭/D B♭ F/C C
fi - re. We can burn brigh - ter than the sun. So if by the
Gm 3fr Am Dm C B♭ C F
time the bar clo - ses and you feel like fall - ing down I'll car - ry you home to - night.

Wide Awake

Words & Music by Lukasz Gottwald, Bonnie McKee,
Katy Perry, Martin Max & Henry Russell Walter

Csus4/G
B♭sus2
F
Csus4
-wake.) 1. Yeah, I was in the dark. I was fall-ing hard with an o-pen heart. (I'm wide a-
-wake.) 2. Not los-ing an-y sleep I picked up ev-'ry piece and land-ed on my feet. (I'm wide a-
-wake.) How did I read the stars so wrong? (I'm wide a-
-wake.) Need noth-ing to com-plete my-self, no. (I'm wide a-
-wake.) And now it's clear to me that ev-'ry-thing you see ain't al-ways what it seems. (I'm wide a-
-wake.) Yeah, I am born a-gain, out of the li-on's den. I don't have to pre-tend. (And it's too
-wake.) Yeah, I was dream-ing for so long.
late...) The sto-ry's o-ver now, the end.
I wish I knew

Csus4/G
B♭sus2
F
Csus4
Csus4/G
B♭sus2
then what I know now. Would-n't dive in, would-n't bow down. Gra-vi-ty hurts. You made it so sweet till I woke
F
Csus4
Csus4/G
B♭sus2
F
Csus4
up on, on the con-crete. Fall - ing from cloud nine,
Csus4/G
B♭sus2
F
Csus4
Csus4/G
B♭sus2
crash - ing from the high. I'm let - ting go to - night.
F
Csus4
Csus4/G
B♭sus2
F
Csus4
Yeah, I'm fall - ing from cloud nine. (I'm wide a-

Csus4/G
B♭sus2
F
Csus4
-wake.) Thun - der rum - bl - ing, cas - tles crum - bl - ing,
(I'm wide a -
Csus4/G
B♭sus2
F
Csus4
Csus4/G
B♭sus2
I am try - ing to hold on. (I'm wide a- wake.) God knows that I tried
-wake.)
F
Csus4
Csus4/G
B♭sus2
F
Csus4
see - ing the bright side. But I'm not blind an - y - more... I'm wide a-
(I'm wide a- wake.)

Csus4/G Bbsus2 F Csus4
-wake. I'm wide a-
Csus4/G Bbsus2 F Csus4 N.C.
-wake. Yeah, I'm
Csus4/G Bbsus2 F Csus4 Csus4/G Bbsus2
fall - ing from cloud nine, crash - ing from the high
F Csus4 Csus4/G Bbsus2
You know I'm let - ting go to - night.

F Csus4 Csus4/G B♭sus2 F Csus4
I'm fall - ing from cloud nine.
I'm wide a-
Csus4/G B♭sus2 F Csus4 Csus4/G B♭sus2
-wake.
I'm wide a - wake.
F Csus4 Csus4/G B♭sus2 F Csus4
I'm wide a - wake.
I'm wide a-
Csus4/G B♭sus2 F Csus4
N.C.
-wake.
I'm wide a - wake.

Wings

Words & Music by Mischke Butler, Michelle Lewis, Thomas Barnes, Peter Kelleher,
Benjamin Kohn, Iain James, Erika Nuri, Jessica Nelson, Jade Thirlwall,
Leigh-Anne Pinnock, Heidi Rojas & Perrie Edwards

Em
N.C.
feet, feet can't touch the ground and I can't hear a
2. I'm fir-ing up on that run-way. I know we're gon-na get there
sound. But you just keep on run-ning up your mouth, yeah.
some-day. But we don't need no read-y, stead-y, go, no.
Em
N.C.
Walk, walk on o-ver
Talk, talk turns in-to
there 'cause I'm too fly to care. Oh, yeah.
air and I don't e-ven care. Oh, yeah.
Your
Am7
Bm7
Cmaj7
words don't mean a thing. I'm not lis-ten-ing. Keep talk-ing,
They're just like

D
Em
all I know is… Ma-ma told me not to waste my life, she said
wat-er off my wings...
G6
D(sus2)
"Spread your wings my lit-tle but-ter-fly. Don't let what they say keep you
C
D(sus2)
up at night. And they can't de-tain you 'cause wings are made to fly."
E
G
And we don't let no-bod-y bring us down. No

D
mat-ter what you say, it won't hurt me. Don't mat-ter if I fall from the sky.
C6
To Coda
D(sus2)
These wings are made to fly.
1.
E
N.C.
2.
E
N.C.
I don't need no one say-ing hey, hey, hey, hey. I don't hear no one say-ing
hey, hey, hey, hey, hey, hey, hey, hey. You bet-ter keep on walk - ing. I don't wan-na hear your talk - ing, boy.

D.S. al Coda
You bet-ter keep on walk - ing.
I don't wan-na hear your talk - ing. Your
Coda
D(sus4)
N.C.
wings are made_ to fly.___
And we don't let___ no-bod - y bring us
Drums
down.___
No mat-ter what_ you say,_ it won't hurt___ me.
Don't mat-ter if___ I fall___ from the sky.___
These wings are made_ to fly.___

1 2 3 4 5 6 7 8 9